T0065530

A GUIDE FOR
WOMEN
IN LEADERSHIP

Fulfilling God's Agenda while Navigating the Workplace

MARY FINCH

WESTBOW
PRESS®
A DIVISION OF THOMAS NELSON
& ZONDERVAN

WestBow Press books may be ordered through booksellers or by contacting:

WestBow Press
A Division of Thomas Nelson & Zondervan
1663 Liberty Drive
Bloomington, IN 47403
www.westbowpress.com
844-714-3454

ISBN: 978-1-6642-0905-3 (sc)
ISBN: 978-1-6642-0906-0 (e)

Library of Congress Control Number: 2020920275

Print information available on the last page.

WestBow Press rev. date: 11/10/2020

ACKNOWLEDGMENTS

When I think of His goodness and blessings, this is enough for me to give thanks to our Lord. The world around us can make us feel incapable, but I am thankful for the consistent encouragement of my wonderful husband. I remember randomly telling him I couldn't, and his response with no delay was, "You are great. You can!" My God, did I receive that message. This man thinks the world of me, so God, once again, you delivered my prayer and your promise. I love you, Mr. Finch. I am also ever so grateful for my parents, who always continue to be a strong support. Mom and Dad, you always keep me in your prayers and love me unconditionally. I truly thank God for you both. Last, my sister Faye, near and far, you have always been just a phone call away. I appreciate our talks and your encouragement. My family, I love you so much, and I thank God for connecting us as one. I would not be who I am without you. My deepest love and sincerest thanks to you.

CONTENTS

Introduction xiii

1 The Great I Am 1

This chapter was crafted to encourage women on their journey, help them recognize the greatness they have within, and lead them to understand better from where that greatness derives, which is through the connection of our Lord Jesus Christ. As women begin to read this chapter, they will understand the importance of affirmations and speaking over their lives by stating, "I am." God is the greatest I Am. He created us all, and because He is, we are great.

2   Who Is She? The Confident Leader...................... 5

This chapter focuses on being the woman who leaves the people around her guessing who she is based on how she shows up and delivers in the room. Her presence and overall confidence in producing results are based not only on her education, work, or world-related experiences but on the connection she has with Jesus Christ. This allows her to have a spirit that can create unknown competitions without her involvement.

3   Mrs. Know-It-All... 9

Mrs. Know-It-All is a chapter about the self-doubting leader who leads with misinformation and missed opportunities to be her best self; She has not tapped into who she can be by being herself. Due to her inability to fit into every conversation and crowd, she struggles to reach her true potential. The reader will identify with these personality traits and through the grace of God create steps to find herself and be who God has called her to be.

4   The Pretty Determined Leader............................13

This chapter is about a leader who has a connection with God. She prays during breaks and lunch because her relationship with God is airtight. The spiritual leader struggles with the world's conflicts and brings her close-knit relationships into her work environment. In reading this chapter, she will continue to be her best honest self, and she always knows God is with her.

5   The Spiritual Leader 17

This chapter is about the leader Who is grounded in God but struggles to navigate the internal corporate politics at work. Due to daily interactions with dishonesty, unnecessary conflict, and intimidation of others, she finds herself attempting to remain humble in her interactions as she knows inside and outside of work she is a servant leader with a calling and obligation.

6 SOS—Sisters Supporting Sisters 21

The SOS sister is here to save everyone from the world. She is the fixer of all concerns and wants to befriend and support every sister she encounters. In this chapter, we'll see that, as a servant of God providing service to support others, she need not neglect herself. In saving others, she has deflected all of her energy away from self-improvement; therefore, through self-awareness, she needs to gain a closer relationship with God to become her best self and the one who indeed requires saving.

7 Leading from the Back 23

There are many different types of leaders. In some of the organizations, you have middle management and senior leaders. In others, you have the front of the house leaders and back of the house leaders. Regardless of what areas these leaders support, they are all leaders. In this chapter, the leader who is not always customer facing will identify that no matter where she is positioned, she is valuable and exactly where she is supposed to be at this time.

8   Driving Connection (Relationship Building) 27

Leadership can become just a term if you are not engaging and able to make others organically feel the need to connect. This chapter focuses not only on the importance of building relationships but also on how divine connections will set up future opportunities and success. Spiritual connections purposefully put you in the right place at the right time to move you through your journey of life.

9   Rebuilding You 31

When it is all said and done, you must remember to replenish the physical and emotional energy you spend tirelessly, day in and day out, with people and their problems. This chapter is focused on the importance of self-care and how imperative it is. Spend time doing the things that make you happy, like reading, writing, or picking up a hobby, but whatever your way to relax, please incorporate prayer to build and maintain your relationship with God. In God, you will find your peace.

About the Author 37

INTRODUCTION

B eing in a leadership role can be tough; being a
woman in a leadership role can be even tougher.
However, to God be the glory for giving us all the tools
we need to be successful in this life. The position you
hold is not for the weak or weak of heart, but vulnerable
you are not. As a woman of God, living and honoring
God's words while punching the clock to fulfill an
organization's goals can become challenging. In this
Guide for Women in Leadership, you will begin to
identify the female boss you are or the female bosses
you have encountered; in either form, you will start to

understand that conflicts exist. However, through prayer you will continue to lead with the gifts and talents God has awarded you.

> **Pray this prayer with me:** Psalm 46:5 (NIV): "God is within her; she will not fall; God will help her at the break of day."

1

The Great I Am

Greetings, my sisters! I wrote this book with you specifically in mind. This chapter aims to capture your attention as we start our journey discussing events and experiences I've had in my life. As women, we go through very similar situations, whether on the sending or receiving side of things. You might have already identified the type of leader you want to be, and your experiences might have supported you in framing this decision. You might already be in a titled leadership position and want to build your skills. You have identified gaps and are familiar with your strengths, and you want to get to the next level.

Wherever you are on your path, you are at the right

place at the right time. As women, we must learn from one another and connect with the creator during our journey. For you, my sister, I named this chapter "The Great I Am." As we jump into the other sections, I want to encourage you! If you have not started to read daily or listen to affirmations, please be sure to start your day first with prayer. Then use continuous encouragement to help build yourself as a person and as a leader. While you are serving in your community, in your church, or on your job, remember that you are a servant of God helping God's people. So you have a significant obligation.

You are great, you are worthy, you are healthy, and you are confident. You are your sister's keeper, you are brilliant, you are beautiful, and you are so many beautiful things. But you would not have any of those characteristics without the great I Am, which means that you are because God is. You are wonderfully and beautifully made because God made you and created you. He loves you, He promotes you, and He protects you. He has never left you, He will never leave you, and you will have favor because He favors you in all ways imaginable and unimaginable. God never said you wouldn't have trouble, but He did say that weeping may endure for a night but joy cometh in the morning.

Whether your problems last a minute or you have been in a storm for a moment, God will get the glory from your experience and move you past that point in time. I encourage you to create movements that allow for your growth and others' extension by paying it forward. Don't be the moment; be the movement that keeps going, growing, evolving, and building from great to greater and then greater to greatest. Be you, be great, and be encouraged, my sisters, because you are these things and more.

> **Pray this prayer with me:** John 15:5–8 (MSG): "I am the Vine, you are the branches, when you're joined with me and I with you, the relation intimate and organic, the harvest is sure to be abundant. Separated, you can't produce a thing. Anyone who separates from me is deadwood, gathered up and thrown on

the bonfire. But if you make yourselves at home with me and my words are at home in you, you can be sure that whatever you ask will be listened to and acted upon. This is how my Father shows who he is—when you produce grapes, when you mature as my disciples."

2

Who Is She? The Confident Leader

In this chapter, we define what confidence is. The word *confidence* can be defined as the feeling or belief that one can rely on something, or firm trust. The most softly spoken person can be assumed to be the least confident based on his or her tone. Would this behavior lead us to question an assumption of confidence? Or is it a reality? The reality is that most people assume someone's determination is based on their interaction or experience.

Most of our knowledge, if not all, stems from a leader or leaders who have appeared highly confident in quoting or stating things, even without substance or truth. We usually have to fact check those people—we have to "trust but verify." Verifying is not trusting, to eliminate any confusion here. In my experience, I have witnessed leaders who sounded strong in statements and would be aggressive in tone if their methods or processes were questioned. I can tell you now that this is not indicative of a strong leader but more representative of an insecure decision maker.

Lack of confidence can stem from people's lack of knowledge, fear of crowds, inadequate readiness (preparedness), fear of how people see them, or fear of not responding appropriately or correctly if challenged. What I have found helpful is to use positive or perceived negative feedback to enhance my skills and transform them into strengths. Use unfavorable critiques as a source of encouragement to build your confidence in the areas in which you need development. For example, if you receive feedback after a presentation that your voice seemed a bit shaky or you didn't appear to be knowledgeable of the slides (the content), then use this information to improve in the future. While this would not be the type of feedback you would desire to receive, you can grow from this by, before your next presentation, reviewing the content over and over, making the presentation your ownAllow your personality to shine through so your audience enjoys you while listening to the presentation. When going over your performance, try rehearsing it in the mirror so you can watch for facial expressions and pauses and work on your pace and volume. This will assist with the shaky tones during your presentation. Practice once more before your presentation, and be sure to pray, giving God the glory so His people can receive you in the best way possible.

Once you master this presentation, be sure to thank God for always showing up and shining out. Your confidence is on its way. Once you identify what is hindering you, your process will tackle those fears and help you stand as the confident leader you are called to be.

> **Pray this prayer with me:** Psalm 121:1–5 (NIV): "I lift up my eyes to the mountains— where does my help come from? My help comes from the LORD, the

Maker of heaven and earth. He will not let your foot slip—he who watches over you will not slumber; indeed, he who watches over Israel will neither slumber nor sleep. The LORD watches over you—the LORD is your shade at your right hand."

3

Mrs. Know-It-All

I remember working for an organization years ago, and my direct supervisor, who was female, was charismatic and engaging. She could speak to any topic I threw at her, and this is why she embodied the title Mrs. Know-It-All. Now, it is never wrong to speak up on topics, especially when you are knowledgeable. Her ability led me to believe she was extremely well rounded.

After I had sat in multiple meetings with her, she began to talk about the work I managed while supporting a few thousand employees. The first time, I must admit, caught me off guard, not because she was speaking about the process and even outcomes but because she was misrepresenting information that I was accountable for. She stated it incorrectly to multiple people all the time. I realized after receiving calls from senior managers inquiring about the process as it related to my department that I was working harder to make corrections based on the inaccurate information she was sharing, with or without me at the table.

So that I wouldn't appear combative by correcting her at the table among her peers, I decided to have a private conversation with her about it. Behind closed doors, she seemed to be receptive and apologetic. She also mentioned to me that, in her previous experience, she had worked in sales and among a predominately male population. She had to be able to speak to every topic, whether the information was correct or not, so she could be involved in the conversations.

Ladies, this was a thought-provoking moment for me—a moment when I came to realize something that could make every encounter clearer for me. During this moment, I gained insight and a better perspective on how she identified and valued herself, feeling the need to fit in. Now, fitting in is fine, but how we think people view us and the way we display ourselves are seen through two different lenses. Ladies, if this was her thing, I was good with it, but these are dangerous patterns to watch for as they could cause more harm than good.

I challenge you to look at your relationships and identify a Mrs. Know-It-All in your group of friends and on your job. Once you've determined the behaviors that suggest this title, please reflect to ensure that *you* are not the Mrs. Know-It-All in your group. If not, keep an eye open for her (or him) and act accordingly.

> **Pray this prayer with me:** Matthew 6:6 (MSG): "Here's what I want you to do: Find a quiet, secluded place so you won't be tempted to role-play before God. Just be there as simply and honestly you can manage. The focus will shift from you to God, and you will begin to send His grace."

4

The Pretty Determined Leader

F ear is an obstacle to reaching your potential due to the *what if*s and *I can't*s. In this chapter, you will learn to speak and to have a "why not" attitude and an "I am" level of confidence. You will begin to talk about abundance over your life and your situations. Here is where you will desire and discern to leave none of your potential behind.

Have you ever heard the term "Don't you worry your pretty little head" about a topic or something requiring completion? For those of you who haven't, the phrase can be used as an insult to insinuate that someone is incapable of thinking or doing two things at the same time, as an example, walking and chewing gum. When you are a woman in the workplace or a leadership role, you can be underestimated. You have to prove yourself and at times engage in an unknown battle of competition with others. But a woman with knowledge who can walk the talk is feared and poses significant confidence. Preparation can and will lead you to claim your wins. I have learned to accept feedback; your greatest haters are transparent and content with their fears. After all, people will desire what you have but may not be sure how to get it. The point of talking about the criticism and haters is to point out your abilities to improve. Using these as examples, you could be a well-dressed sister and know how to put an outfit together; however, in the office, you have a relaxed dress code, and now you've overheard someone in the office saying that your causal dress seems to be too comfortable. The comment is made that, because you are casually dressed, it's hard to envision you in a position or level any higher than you are in currently. If this is the type of feedback you are hearing, don't take offense. Level up your casual attire from joggers and leggings to business casual, or if you are in an office where your business casual attire does not match the professional office attire, you should begin to dress for the job you want and not the position you have. So level up.

These examples may not fit your situation; however, you can always level up no matter what condition you are in, as you will still receive feedback that feels critical and even hurtful at times. But believe me when I say, "Grow from it. You will glow from it!" Let your work, drive and successful results speak for themselves, and let the naysayers say nay. You don't have to respond verbally to the momentary challenges because your goal is to excel in life, and to do so, you must learn to be receptive to feedback—good, bad, or indifferent—and level up. So, my sisters, I challenge you to leave none of your potential behind and remain determined to excel while claiming your position in life. Being a committed leader can put your faith under pressure, so I leave you with this prayer reminder.

James 1:5–8 (MSG): "If you don't know what you're doing, pray to the Father. He loves to help. You'll get his help, and won't be condescended to when you ask for it. Ask boldly, believingly, without a second thought. People who 'worry their prayers' are like wind-whipped waves. Don't think you're going to get anything from the Master that way, drift at sea, keeping all your options open."

5

The Spiritual Leader

To you, my sister in Christ, prayer should be a natural process throughout your day. Pray when you rise in the morning, pray on your commute to the office (virtual or other), and pray before you enter the doors of your office or before joining your virtual call and group meetings. Have a midday prayer at lunch and an end-of-work prayer, as He has gotten you through the day. If you are a sister with a slick silver tongue, increase your prayer, my sister, so that those around you don't get whiplash from what could be.

Working in my field, supporting employees from day to day, and having multiple difficult conversations, the challenge to encourage, coach, and discuss performance management and conflict resolution can be extremely demanding. A given day might seem straightforward, but there are a lot of personalities and personal outside influences that can transfer to the job. At times, in conversations with employees, mainly depending on the nature of the discussions, I am emotionally accountable for my reaction, not only in the workplace but as a servant to God. I take deep breaths, vent if necessary to my reliable sources, pray, and continue. I make prayer a daily supplement to process my moment and progress in my day. If you establish prayer as a requirement as you do with getting to work and fulfilling your employer's needs, you will see the difference in outcomes. When we pray, asking God for less of us and more of Him, truly requesting that Father God takes over before, during, and after our situations, He shows up powerfully. Just so you know, you might not witness situations He has resolved and blocked on your behalf, but you can count on the fact that He has covered you. My spiritual advice to you as a leader would be to wait and listen to God. Please add prayer to those other assigned duties in your job description; incorporate prayer into your daily routine.

When you are in need, please remember to be encouraged and pay it forward.

- Jehovah-Jireh: "The Lord will provide a sacrifice." (Genesis 22:13–24 NIV)

- Jehovah-Rapha: "The Lord that healeth thee." (Exodus 15:26 NIV)

- Jehovah-Shalom: "The Lord our peace." (Judah 6:24 NIV)

- Jehovah-Nissi: "The Lord our banner." (Exodus 17:8–15 NIV)

- Jehovah-Raah: "The Lord my Shepard." (Psalm 23:1–6 NIV)

- Jehovah-Tsideknu: "The Lord our righteousness." (Jeremiah 23:6 NIV)

Pray this prayer with me: Psalm 37:23–24 (NIV): "The LORD makes firm the steps of the one who delights in him; though he may stumble, he will not fall, for the LORD upholds him with his hand."

6

SOS—Sisters Supporting Sisters

During my experience working for previous employers, I've been fortunate to encounter women I could easy befriend over time. Being a woman of God, my desire to help, encourage, and coach others has been nothing less than a gift From God. I am aware that my service in being a servant has been my greatest win toward blessings and promotions. In short, I know who butters my bread; He is my provider. One of the misconceptions of some women is that we cannot get along. I would amend that statement to say that people with various personalities, agendas, external personal conflicts, and environments have formed, shaped, and developed different worldly views that can create disengagement with others, with the world, and within oneself. So it's not that we can't get along—we can, we have, and we will. As women in leadership, we are constantly under the microscope with the opinion of others' personal views about who they think we should be versus who we are.

Work at getting along with one another and with God. Otherwise, you'll never get as much as a glimpse of God. Make sure no one gets left out of God's generosity. Keep a sharp eye out for weeds of bitter discontent. A thistle or two gone to seed can ruin a whole garden in no time. Watch out for the Esau syndrome: trading away God's lifelong gift in order to satisfy a short-term appetite. You well know how Esau later regretted that impulsive act and wanted God's blessing, but by then it was too late, tears or no tears.

> **Pray this prayer with me:** Philippians 4:7 (NIV): "And the peace of God, which transcends all understanding, will guard your hearts and your minds in Christ Jesus."

7

Leading from the Back

N ot every leader leads from the front of the house, and not every front-house leader is comfortable with leading from the back. Regardless, if you are a leader who is visible in the front or comfortable with leading from the back, you are still an active leader. Some believe that if you are not at the forefront, then you will not get recognized. Yet as a leader, especially one managing a team, you should always acknowledge your players. There is nothing worse than being a part of a work team in any industry, committee, or social group and not recognizing worker bees. Back-of-the-house leaders and frontline workers are essential and definitely should be recognized for their contributions. On some occasions, in my experience, the person working behind the scenes contributes effortlessly to hold things together. If you are leading from behind the scenes but not by choice, I encourage you to demonstrate to your manager how you are prepared to take your career to the next level.

The first step would be to create a business case with clear examples reflecting your contributions and growth. Second, schedule time with him or her and discuss your interest in career advancement. Be prepared to outline efforts you have led as an individual contributor and any projects you actively supported as a team member, helping the team's success. Before you have this conversation with your leader, be sure to have the meeting before the meeting. Be sure to connect with God before taking action to make your request known to Him, who will fulfill your heart's desires in due time. The Bible states in Philippians 4:6–8 (NIV): "Do not be anxious about anything, but in every situation, by prayer and petition, with thanksgiving, present your requests to God. And the peace of God, which transcends all understanding, will guard your hearts and your minds in Christ Jesus.

Finally, brothers and sisters, whatever is true, whatever is noble, whatever is right, whatever is pure, whatever is lovely, whatever is admirable—if anything is excellent or praiseworthy—think about such things."

"I charge you to step into your calling and claim your blessings. If you are behind the scenes or ready to take the step toward leadership, be honest, have patience with yourself, and understand that the process takes time. Pray during the process and step into your calling, my sister.

8

Driving Connection (Relationship Building)

While the chapters leading to this section are essential, I am personally excited about the topic of relationship. Let's look at the word *relationship*. It can be defined as how two or more concepts, objects, or people are connected, or the state of being connected. As we discussed in a previous chapter, "Leading from the Back," the identification of a leader is not only based on the title but demonstrated through how a person interacts with or handles someone or a situation. Yes, in managing people, it is crucial to understand how to meet people where they are. Listening to them, communicating with them, and understanding who they are in the moment will potentially reveal to you who they are throughout most of your interactions. Your relationships will vary from work related, friendships, partnerships, spousal, church related, and even social organizations, but on all of those platforms, regardless of who the person might be, your relationships derive from some connection that you and that person share. Links come to an end due to a lack of respect or trust.

In the workplace, you might not have personal conflict. Allow your work reputation to speak for your work product, but don't get wrapped up in the team conflict or personality differences, people are entitled to be different and work differently than you.. If there is a group assignment and your colleague owns his or her part, wherever the gaps might be, it builds trust and healthy relationships when you can step up in a situation to support in that area. In the workplace or outside of it, it is essential for you as a leader to build not only relationships but trustworthy relationships in your career. Don't become discouraged if every work relationship is not favorable, you cannot win them all.

It is essential to have relationships and trust people as you grow as an individual. As a reminder, spiritually, the most critical bond you will need to develop is the one with God.

John 14:27 (NIV): "Peace I leave with you; my peace I give you. I do not give to you as the world gives. Do not let your hearts be troubled and do not be afraid."

9

Rebuilding You

In Romans 14:1–5 (NIV), we read,

> Accept the one whose faith is weak, without
> quarreling over disputable matters. One
> person's faith allows them to eat anything,
> but another, whose faith is weak, eats only
> vegetables. The one who eats everything
> must not treat with contempt the one who
> does not, and the one who does not eat
> everything must not judge the one who
> does, for God has accepted them. Who
> are you to judge someone else's servant?
> To their own master, servants stand or fall.

And they will stand, for the Lord is able to make them stand.

As we discussed in previous chapters about the personality types related to women in leadership, whether you identify as any of the kinds of leaders I've encountered or you have met, the most essential message of all is to pray. Pray for those who lift you up and those who spite you. With so many things within ourselves and within the world, we don't know why people behave the way they do. Our life experiences play a significant role in how we carry out our days and in our interactions with people within our days; therefore, pray for yourselves and others. Pray for covering, asking God to cover their hearts and minds to find peace and find themselves in their journey. While their battles might not be yours, you can face the challenges that feel like yours to conquer and resolve. If the above is your battle, my sister, I pray for peace, peace of mind, harmony in relationships, peace in your journey, and peace in being still to wait and hear from our God. Life's challenges can be hard, whether work, home, or personal, but remember, my sister, you are healthy and well even when you might think you are weak. Self-care is a must, so indulge in time to make yourself feel good. Get that pedicure, manicure, massage, or acupuncture, even therapy if you need to talk it out. Take time for yourself to notice the small things in life. Seek the Lord our God, and remember what a breeze feels like during the fall months and how it looks when the trees start to create an ambiance of colors more decorative than a freshly painted portrait. Remember love and how God felt when He created you in your mother's womb, forming your eyes, nose, and mouth in such a short period. While the world can be hard, no one will ever adore, cherish, and love you forever like our Lord thy God. When you think of love, think of Him because he gave you life. He is the reason you live and breathe, and He will see you through any and all challenges. When you see a rainbow in the sky, remember God's promise to you. He is always with you, and He loves you; therefore, remember to love others with the love of God.

Prayers for you.

As we close out the book, I leave you with prayers to support you now and along your journey.

Faith	Psalm 119:11 (NIV)
	"I have hidden your word in my heart that I might not sin against you."
Trust	Matthew 6:30–33 (NIV)
	"If that is how God clothes the grass of the field, which is here today and tomorrow is thrown into the fire, will he not much more clothe you—you of little faith? So do not worry, saying, 'What shall we eat?' or 'What shall we drink?' or 'What shall we wear?' For the pagans run after all these things, and your heavenly Father knows that you need them. But seek first his kingdom and his righteousness, and all these things will be given to you as well."

Character   Jeremiah 29:13–14 (MSG)

"When you come looking for me, you'll find me. Yes, when you get serious about finding me and want it more than anything else, I'll make sure you won't be disappointed. GOD's DECREE. I'll turn things around for you. I'll bring you back from all the countries into which I drove you— GOD's DECREE—bring you home to the place from which I sent you off into exile. You can count on it."

Relationship   John 15:7–8 (MSG)

"I am the Vine, you are the branches. When you're joined with me and I with you, the relation intimate and organic, the harvest is sure to be abundant. Separated, you can't produce a thing. Anyone who separates from me is deadwood, gathered up and thrown on the bonfire. But if you make yourselves at home with me and my words are at home in you, you can be sure that whatever you ask will be listened to and acted upon."

Leadership	Proverbs 3:5–6 (MSG)
	"Trust GOD from the bottom of your heart; don't try to figure out everything on your own. Listen for God's voice in everything you do, everywhere you go; he's the one who will keep you on track."
Health	Psalm 37:4 (NIV)
	"Take delight in the LORD, and he will give you the desires of your heart."

ABOUT THE AUTHOR

Mary Finch is a woman of God, wife, daughter, and professional who feels most accomplished by serving others to develop and obtain their growth potential.

Mary was born and raised on the south side of Chicago. As a product of Chicago public schools, Mary furthered her education by attending a historically black college to earn a bachelor's in business administration in management and finance. She continued her education to earn a master's in business administration in information technology. Mary has also studied organizational psychology, and she used these skills for twenty-plus years in human resources, specializing in conflict resolution and employee relations. As a Certified Master Life Coach, Mary supports people in the areas of Confidence, Spirituality, Business Coaching in personal and professional development as well as relationship life coaching. The work Mary contributes toward career coaching led to this guide. As an African American woman in Leadership, she has identified many different leadership types. As a woman striving for self-improvement, Mary understands that God is her driving force to accomplish all things desired and designed by and through Him.

Printed in the United States
By Bookmasters